Special Diets

Gluten-Free Diets

by Mari Schuh

Consulting Editor: Gail Saunders-Smith, PhD

Consultant:
Amy L. Lusk, MS, RD, LD
Registered Dietitian

CAPSTONE PRESS
a capstone imprint

Pebble Plus is published by Capstone Press,
1710 Roe Crest Drive, North Mankato, Minnesota 56003.
www.capstonepub.com

Library of Congress Cataloging-in-Publication Data
Schuh, Mari C., 1975–
Gluten-free diets / by Mari Schuh
     pages cm. — (Pebble plus. Special diets)
Audience: Age 4-8.
Audience: Grades K to 3.
Includes bibliographical references and index.
ISBN 978-1-4914-0589-5 (library binding : alk. paper)
ISBN 978-1-4914-0623-6 (eBook pdf)
1. Gluten-free diet—Juvenile literature. I. Title.
RM237.86.S34 2015
641.5'638—dc23   2014001858

Editorial Credits
Shelly Lyons, editor; Heidi Thompson, designer; Kelly Garvin, media researcher;
     Katy LaVigne, production specialist

Photo Credits
All photos by Capstone Studios/Karon Dubke

Note to Parents and Teachers

The Special Diets series supports national science standards related to health and nutrition. This
book describes and illustrates some foods that fit and don't fit into a gluten-free diet. The images
support early readers in understanding the text. The repetition of words and phrases helps early
readers learn new words. This book also introduces early readers to subject-specific vocabulary
words, which are defined in the Glossary section. Early readers may need assistance to read some
words and to use the Table of Contents, Glossary, Read More, Internet Sites, and Index sections
of the book.

Printed in the United States of America in North Mankato, Minnesota
032014   008087CGF14

Table of Contents

Who Needs a Gluten-Free Diet?

Gluten is found in grains.

Some people can't eat grain

that has gluten in it.

They have gluten intolerances.

Eat This, Not That

Most bread has gluten in it.

People who can't eat gluten

can eat gluten-free bread.

This bread is often made

with rice flour or potato flour.

Instead of wheat crackers,
they can eat rice cakes
or corn chips. Rice and corn
do not have gluten.

People can enjoy quinoa
instead of pasta.
Quinoa is a gluten-free seed
and is full of nutrients.

Instead of cake
they can enjoy ice cream.
Adults can also bake
a gluten-free cake.

Lots of foods have gluten.

Adults can check food labels.

They can look for gluten-free foods.

People who can't eat gluten
can enjoy fruits and vegetables.
Meat, fish, nuts, and seeds
are gluten-free too.

What's a Reaction?

People with a gluten intolerance

feel sick after eating gluten.

They might feel tired

or have stomach pain.

They may get an itchy rash.

How to Be a Friend

Kids must watch

what they eat. But they

still want to have fun.

Be a friend and

have fun with them!

Safe Recipe
Yogurt Parfait

What You Need

1 tbsp. (15mL) golden raisins
1 tbsp. (15 mL) nuts
1 cup (240 mL) fruit-flavored
    yogurt or Greek yogurt
½ cup (120 mL) berries, such as
    strawberries, blueberries,
    or raspberries

What You Do

Mix raisins and nuts into yogurt. Put half of the yogurt mixture in a tall glass. Top with half of the berries. Put the rest of the yogurt mixture on top of the layer of berries. Place the rest of the berries on top as the last layer. Enjoy a yummy, gluten-free yogurt parfait!

Makes 1 serving

Glossary

gluten—a protein found in wheat, barley, rye, and some other grains

grain—the seed of a cereal plant, such as wheat, rice, corn, oats, or barley

intolerance—not being able to eat certain foods without becoming ill

label—a list on food packages that shows what the food is made of

nutrient—a part of a food, like a vitamin, that is used for growth

pasta—a food made from flour and water that is made into shapes and dried

quinoa (KEEN-wah)—seeds that are used as food and ground into flour

rash—itchy spots or red patches on the skin caused by an allergy or illness

Read More

Kruszka, Bonnie J. *Eating Gluten-Free with Emily: A Story for Children with Celiac Disease.* Bethesda, Md.: Woodbine House, 2004.

London, Melissa. *The GF Kid: A Celiac Disease Survival Guide.* Bethesda, Md: Woodbine House, 2005.

Tuminelly, Nancy. *Cool Wheat-Free Recipes: Delicious & Fun Foods Without Gluten.* Cool Recipes for Your Health. Minneapolis: Abdo Publishing, 2013.

Internet Sites

FactHound offers a safe, fun way to find Internet sites related to this book. All of the sites on FactHound have been researched by our staff.

Here's all you do:
Visit *www.facthound.com*
Type in this code: 9781491405895

Index

Super-cool stuff! Check out projects, games and lots more at
www.capstonekids.com

Critical Thinking Using the Common Core

1. Healthy foods are an important part of a gluten-free diet.
   What are some healthy foods that you can include in your diet?
   (Key Ideas and Details)

2. What are some of the foods that can be included in a gluten-free diet?
   (Key Ideas and Details)

Word Count: 175
Grade: 1
Early-Intervention Level: 16